"Lisa Shea's little gem, 'How to Wait Well,' is full of hard-won wisdom, spiritual truth, and a heart that longs to revere Jesus. Each day you'll receive a nugget of wisdom, along with a powerful prayer. A great way to spend 30 days!"

*Mary DeMuth, author of 'Jesus Every Day'*

"Grab a cup of tea, a blanket, and 'How to Wait Well', and curl up with the goodness of God. Lisa's devotional will take you on a journey to the heart of the Father, revealing how much He loves you. I highly recommend this book to anyone who is in need of a 30-day reminder of how much you are loved. You will read this time and time again when you need a pick me up! Enjoy the adventure!"

*Debbie Hancock, Founder/President of Compassion To Act*

"Is waiting easy? No. A thousand times, no. But it is in the waiting where we can quiet ourselves to experience the Living God moving in our midst... Lisa's 30-day devotional will shake the dust off the word you may have lost or disbelieved, and bring life to dead bones!"

*Ish Payne, Restoring Hearts Ministries*

# Hope in Christ
## Romans 15:13

# How to
# Wait Well

## 30 WAYS TO EXPERIENCE GOD

# How to Wait Well

## 30 WAYS TO EXPERIENCE GOD

# LISA SHEA

All rights reserved. This book is protected under the copyright laws of the United States of America. This book may not be copied or reprinted for commercial gain or profit. The use of short quotations or occasional page copying for personal or group study is permitted and encouraged. Permission will be granted upon request.

Scripture quotations are from the ESV® Bible (The Holy Bible, English Standard Version®), copyright © 2001 by Crossway, a publishing ministry of Good News Publishers. Used by permission. All rights reserved.

Scripture quotations marked (NIV) are taken from the Holy Bible, New International Version®, NIV®. Copyright © 1973, 1978, 1984 by Biblica, Inc.TM Used by permission of Zondervan. All rights reserved worldwide. www.zondervan.com

ISBN-13: 9781075726927

**How To Wait Well**

By Lisa Shea

© Copyright 2019 by **Lisa Shea**

Designed by Kim Hall

# Dedication

Mike, Sydney, Samantha & Matthew, you all make my heart smile. I love you all more than you know! May the Truths in this devotional stay with you forever.

Dad & Mom, (Jim & Dotty Thompson) thank you for making so many dreams come true! I thank God for giving me the best parents anyone could ask for!

To those who helped me edit this devotional, especially Ramona Pedemonte, my heartfelt thanks!

Lord God, there aren't enough words to express my gratitude to You. Anoint the words on these pages to change lives, all for Your Glory.

# Table of Contents

Welcome ............................................................................. v

How To Use This Devotional ............................................. vii

Before We Begin ................................................................. ix

Day 1: *God is Faithful God* ..................................................1

Day 2: *God is a Source of Strength* .........................................5

Day 3: *God is Powerful* ........................................................9

Day 4: *God is a Help in Trouble* ..........................................13

Day 5: *God is Almighty* .....................................................17

Day 6: *God is my Support* ..................................................21

Day 7: *God is the Lord our Maker* ......................................25

Day 8: *God is the Lord Who Heals You* ...............................29

Day 9: *God is the Lord Who Provides* ..................................33

Day 10: *God is Gracious* ....................................................37

Day 11: *God is the God Who Sees Me* .................................41

Day 12: *God the Lord is Peace* ............................................45

Day 13: *God is the Strength of My Heart* .............................49

Day 14: *God is a Mighty God* ............................................53

Day 15: *God is Near* .........................................................57

Day 16: *God is My Rock* .................................................. 61

Day 17: *God is My Righteous Father* ..................................... 65

Day 18: *God of Retribution* .............................................. 69

Day 19: *God is Abundant in Power* ........................................ 73

Day 20: *God is my Strong Deliverer* ...................................... 77

Day 21: *God is my Hope and Trust* ........................................ 81

Day 22: *God Can Do More than All We Ask* ................................. 85

Day 23: *God is the Father of Compassion* ................................. 89

Day 24: *God is a Stronghold* ............................................. 93

Day 25: *God is a Source of Strength* ..................................... 97

Day 26: *God Sustains Me* ................................................. 101

Day 27: *God is My Confidence* ............................................ 105

Day 28: *God is the Eternal King* ......................................... 109

Day 29: *God is a Refuge* ................................................. 113

Day 30: *God is My Redeemer* .............................................. 117

Moving Forward: *God Covers You* .......................................... 121

Only Through Jesus ........................................................ 123

Devotional Themes ......................................................... 124

# Welcome!

I am so excited that you are sharing the next 30 days with me. Through being in ministry for many years, there are several areas in life about which I have become passionate. It wasn't until recently that I realized each of these areas centered on the same underlying theme: our knowledge of God. I am embarrassed to say that it took me awhile to discover this; but hey, we are all a work in progress!

The Lord highlighted to me, through my own life and through those to whom I have ministered, a common lack of faith and trust in the person of God. How we handle any situation, good or bad, is in direct relation to our belief in Him. Whether we have been Christians for fifty years or five minutes, we all must grow in our awareness of the Truth of who He is. His Truth. What does the Bible say about Him? His Word, regarding His character, must supersede our experience or our lack of experience with Him.

It is so easy to proclaim how great God is when life is good. It is also easy to affirm His greatness when we experience a breakthrough after a challenging season. But what are we like during the hard seasons? How do we think, feel, and act in the midst of a trial?

Some of you may find it easy or natural to praise God during a difficult season. That is great! Many of us though, really struggle when things get hard. Until we experience our own breakthrough, our times of trial can go two ways. We can worry, or we can try to control things. Yet, if we learn to wait well, we can experience God's promises for ourselves, in a peaceful state. We will then come to know our God in a new way, gaining incredible strength in Him.

Psalm 91:4 (NIV) says, "He will cover you with His feathers, and under his wings you will find refuge; His faithfulness will be your shield and rampart."

God cares about every detail of your life. He loves you, protects you and provides for you in every situation. That is hard to believe, sometimes, when life is tough and we are waiting for a change to occur. But it is the Truth. May the scriptures in this devotional help you to realize that you are covered with the gentle feathers and powerful wings of the Almighty God. In all situations, you will find refuge. He promises you that!

# How to Use This Devotional

Each day of this devotional begins with a scriptural attribute of God, along with an accompanying Bible verse. Meditate, memorize, write, reflect on and speak the verse out loud for each day.

Continue daily by reading each day's scripture and devotion. Finish your time by using the prayer provided to start your own conversation with God. Be aware that God may show you that particular characteristic of Himself. Journaling your experiences will provide insight and give you an opportunity to hear from God for yourself.

Romans 10:17 says, "…faith comes from hearing and hearing through the word of Christ." By spending time focusing on who God is according to His Word, we build our faith. It also is a form of praise. These words are the Sword of the Spirit and they will put the enemy on notice about whom we trust. Declaring the Word of God over your situation will help you focus on Him, drawing your eyes to the One fighting on your behalf rather than on the fight itself.

Distraction leads to deception. If you allow your circumstances, whether significant or minor, to sway your thoughts and emotions away from God, then you can wind up on a path of deception. Many opportunities for God to turn a very painful situation into good are missed because we become distracted and ultimately deceived. We start to believe lies, such as "things won't change," or "God doesn't care about me." Don't let those lies outweigh the Truth of His powerful promises. Again, in the words of Psalm 94:1, as you wait, He will cover you with His feathers, and under His wings you will find refuge; His faithfulness will be your shield.

# Before We Begin

*"He says, "Be still and know that I am God. I will be exalted among the nations, I will be exalted in the earth!"*

Psalm 46:10

As I came across this scripture during a time of waiting (quite painful waiting, I might add) the words "and know" jumped out at me. I began to pay more attention to the "and know" part of the verse than to the "be still" part. If you have been a church attendee for any length of time, you may know that "be still" is a common fall back phrase. When we don't know what to do, it seems someone throws out, "Oh, just be still…" I don't know about you, but what does that even look like?

As I studied this, I discovered that the Hebrew word for "know" is Yada (pronounced Yaw-da). Yada means to recognize, admit, acknowledge, declare, understand and experience. "To experience," that was it!

Now look at the verse again: "Be still and *experience* God." Being still doesn't mean you crawl into bed, pull the covers over your head, and lay motionless. It means to be still in your spirit and watch God move. Action may be required to follow His instruction; obedience always carries a blessing. As you do your part, you will experience God doing what only He can do. After all, He is an expert in the miraculous!

In order to wait well, there are several things we should do. First, and most importantly, we must experience God through His Word. Second, we experience Him through what He has done for us. All personal experiences, however, must align with scripture (Acts 17:11). Finally, we experience Him through what He has done for others (Revelation 12:11).

I've noticed that we tend to trust God in areas in which He has already shown up. For example, if you have experienced a miracle in your marriage, as I have, you know He can change *any* relationship, no matter what condition it is in. God is the Restorer (Deuteronomy 30:3). If you have been physically healed, you know Him as Healer (Exodus 15:26). Did He deliver you from an addiction? You know, that you know, that He is the Deliverer (Psalm 18:2). If you've trusted God with your finances and the money always shows up on time, you know Him as Provider (Philippians 4:19).

Think about this, though; you know Him as having one of these characteristics as a direct result of what happened to you. You experienced Him! But how strong is your faith in areas where you haven't experienced Him in action yet?

Now I know what some of you may be saying. "Lisa, I trusted God as _____ (you fill in the blank). He didn't do what I thought He should. Things didn't turn out like I expected."

I understand that when things don't turn out like we believe they could, it seems as though God ignored us. Our hope is dashed; our trust is broken; our faith is damaged.

For example, I was part of a prayer team that diligently, fervently, passionately, and consistently prayed for a young child to be healed of cancer. The child even insisted Jesus would heal her. Prophetic words were received that she would be healed. Imagine the blow to our faith when she wasn't.

We can easily admit she was healed when she got to heaven. Of course people are fully healed in heaven. We knew that before we started praying for this child. Let's be honest; our prayers were that she would be healed here on earth. Just imagine the testimony of God as Healer for her family, our church and our city if He healed this child on earth! It made perfect sense that He would want to demonstrate His power that way. God has healed people with cancer before, but that isn't what happened this time. Were we devastated? Yes! Did our faith falter? Yes. Did we question Him? Yes!

We had to ask ourselves, "Is God still Healer?" The answer is yes, He is. The scriptures declare it, and that is the proof a resilient Christian should stand on. There are many instances that can lead you to question God's power. Maybe you believed for an upturn in your business and trusted God would provide, but you ended up in bankruptcy. Is He still your Provider? The answer is again: Yes, He certainly is!

Negative experiences are where our faith-walks need strengthening. We cannot allow a negative experience, or one that we don't understand, to override the Truth of God's Word. Do I still pray for the sick to be healed? YES! Why? Because He is the One who heals (Exodus 15:26) and numerous scriptures tell us to pray for the sick. Guess what? I have seen people healed since that precious little girl went to heaven. Some were healed over time and some instantly. I have personally experienced God as Healer.

Do I understand why some are healed, and others are not? Why some receive financial breakthrough before the bottom falls out and others don't? Why some are freed from addictions and others still struggle? No, I don't understand. But I refuse to let a negative experience, one that seemingly negates God's Word, keep me from believing Him. So, what do we say when things don't work out as we hoped? We simply declare, "I don't know why this happened like this. Maybe someday I will. I don't understand it, but I choose to trust God anyway. He is good and He covers me." Be still and KNOW (YADA) that he is God, that He is good, no matter what.

There comes a point in time when we just need to make a decision. It is much easier to resolve this *before* hardship hits, but it is a decision that must be made, nonetheless. Be firm that no matter what comes your way, you will allow God to work in you and through you. No matter how the enemy attempts to trip you up, be determined that it will not kill your faith. Then, when you have survived the storm, you can share what God did and what He taught you. Isn't that the best way to refute the enemy who created the calamity in your life? Let God redeem the situation and then praise Him for it! Afterwards, you can go and encourage others with your testimony of a faithful God (Revelation 12:11).

May this 30-day devotional give you the encouragement you need. God's Word is sharper than any two-edged sword (Hebrews 4:12). It is the only offensive weapon in the armor of God (Ephesians 6:17), and it will not return empty (Isaiah 55:11).

Spend time listening to Him as you pray the prayers each day. Don't be afraid to ask the Lord to reveal Himself to you. He wants you to experience who He really is. Just pay attention. Sometimes a revelation will be subtle; other times it will be mind-blowingly obvious. Let Him out of the box you may have put Him in. In other words, don't limit God. He is so much bigger and better than we think. Be open to a fresh and new revelation of who He is.

# DAY 1

## God is a Faithful God

Deuteronomy 32:4

*I can do all things through Him
who strengthens me.*

Philippians 4:13

I remember a time I was extremely weary and frequently to the point of tears. I was trying very hard to do what I felt God was asking me to do. In this case, it was being respectful to my husband when our marriage was a disaster. My last hope, which should have been my first and only hope, was a move of Almighty God.

But I was tired. There were no discernable results from my obedience to Ephesians 5:33, which called me to be a respectful wife. I was making a last-ditch effort to save my marriage and it seemed nothing was changing. I felt hopeless and wanted to quit trying.

One particular morning as I sat at a red light with tears filling my eyes, a runner crossed the street in front of me. As she ran past, I experienced God. On the back of her T-shirt was written:

*"I can do all things through Him
who strengthens me."*

God knew my heart. He saw my despair, and He encouraged me with His word. Isn't it ironic? He used a runner to encourage me to keep moving. What a precious reminder that, when I felt I couldn't continue, Jesus would fortify me. I would be able to do what He asked me to do in my marriage, and I could trust that He would work it out.

*Lord, I give you this day. Glory to your name. As we transition to Richmond, Lord lessen the burden on my children, teach me to love them as they need - to speak the tone of love and caring as they need. Lord remove any thoughts planted before them to go against your will. Lord reveal your truths to them, Alexis, Kailin AJ & Levi*

## Prayer

*Jesus, I want to experience You in a real way today. When I am weak or discouraged, You promise to give me strength. I thank You for that promise and stand on it today! Your Word has power, and I am eager to see what You will do in my life as I allow You to work in me. In Your name, amen.*

- I ask for a sign you are working things out for food, a word, a call, a visit, a mention of you.

- I ask to remove the hard shell of Lexi and cover her in your grace

- I ask AJ to not be compromised or burdened by this move.

- I ask for Kailin to seek you - as He sees us obey you.

# DAY 2

## God is a Source of Strength

Isaiah 28:6

*And let us not grow weary of doing good, for in due season we will reap, if we do not give up.*

Galatians 6:9

The Bible tells us that, because of the joy set before Him, Jesus endured the cross (Hebrews 12:2). Jesus had unwavering faith in His Father. He trusted Him even to the point of death. God has proven Himself faithful to the faithful (Psalm 18:25).

If we set a goal beforehand to obey and honor God in the midst of a trial, it becomes easier to press through when we would rather pass out. In other words, in anticipation of the joy of reaping, we can endure this season. Continuing to do good when we don't see immediate results is hard. It is easy to grow discouraged.

The faith you possess when walking through challenges is directly related to who you believe God to be. If He promises that you will reap a good harvest when the time is right, then, as you do your part, you will see Him fulfill this promise. Don't give up!

## HOW TO WAIT WELL

*Lord you know my current state - trusting your promises and not the circumstance is much more soothing. Your strength brings me comfort. Richmond Virginia here we come - sights unseen, jobs unknown, yet we know all will be fulfilled as promises from the Lord. God fill me with anticipation*

## Prayer

*Lord, help me to see beyond my circumstances to Your purposes. When I get tired and discouraged, please breathe fresh life into me. I ask for the Holy Spirit to empower me to press on and not quit. I pray for the faith to persevere. I want to see what You accomplish through this situation for my good and for Your glory. In Jesus' name, amen.*

# DAY 3

# God is a Great and Powerful God

Jeremiah 32:18

> *Now to Him who is able to do far more abundantly than all that we ask or think, according to the power at work within us…*
>
> Ephesians 3:20

Isn't it encouraging to know that God can do more than we can even imagine? He can resurrect any situation, or He can change hearts about that situation. He is *that* big. The problem we have is that we start viewing our personal case through our own eyes and limited understanding. When we shift our perspective, though, to God's infinite power and His promises for His children, our outlook shifts from bleak to beautiful.

In what situation are you awaiting change? Speak Ephesians 3:20 over it. You can say something like this: "Lord, I celebrate that you know every detail of my situation, including matters of which I am unaware. Thank you that you can do more in this than I can could ever imagine. I make the decision to trust and rest in you today, knowing you are able to do abundantly more."

# HOW TO WAIT WELL

*10/9/2020*

*Lord you can see to the depths of an Ocean - your vision is infinite - your love endures. Lord unfold and show us our home - show us our assignment clear so we don't question the what or the how. Lord reveal your love to Xailin & Lexi.*

## Prayer

*Father, I ask for a revelation of Your perfect love today. Speak to me in such a way that I know what concerns me, concerns You. I believe I can persevere because Your Word says that You have me in the palm of Your hand (John 10:28). I ask You to reveal Your mighty power in my life as I honor You through obedience. In Jesus' name, amen.*

# DAY 4

# God is Our Help in Trouble

Psalm 46:1

*But they who wait for the Lord shall renew their strength;*
*they shall mount up with wings*
*like eagles; they shall run and not be weary;*
*they shall walk and not faint.*

Isaiah 40:31

There are times when we feel like we are falling instead of flying. We become overwhelmed with our lives, and we can't seem to catch a break. I remember the time a Christian counselor told me to throw my husband out of the house to get his attention. I did not have biblical grounds to do that, and I was not in any physical danger. How hopeless I felt!

As I drove home from the appointment, crying, asking God to help me, I heard the still small voice say, "Don't do that. Be still." It was as if God breathed peace and strength into my heart. I felt that He heard my cry. I was renewed to keep fighting for my marriage. I didn't know what the solution would look like, but throwing my husband out wasn't the answer. My faith was renewed as I waited for God to lead the way. He did!

Shortly after I felt God say, "Be still," I received biblical tools that equipped me for the challenge to restore my marriage. A book called "Motivating Your Man God's Way" by Dr. Emerson and Sarah Eggerichs arrived in my mailbox from a friend who knew nothing about my failing marriage. I mean, nothing!

Once again, I experienced God as He provided me with instructions. God showed me He is a loving Father. He heard me, and He answered me. He will do that for you too.

## Prayer

*Father God, renew my strength as I wait for Your direction. Speak to me in a tangible way today. Help me to know that I matter to You and that You are present, ready to show me what to do next! Guide me in Your ways. Help me to do my part so that You can do a miraculous work in my heart. In Jesus' name, amen.*

# DAY 5

# God is an Almighty God

Genesis 17:1

*Trust in the Lord with all your heart, and do not lean on your own understanding. In all your ways acknowledge him, and he will make straight your paths.*

Proverbs 3:5-6

From the beginning of my second marriage, Proverbs 3:5-6 sat displayed in a whitewashed frame in my home reminding me of God's faithfulness. After a painful divorce when I was younger and still without children, God had healed my heart and had given me another chance at marriage; a happy one this time. Because I had experience with God making my path straight, I trusted Him. Or so I thought.

As the years went by, the frame became merely an object to dust and the verse sadly overlooked. When life got bad, I forgot to trust. I fell back to trying to make sense of things from my own perspective. Proverbs 3:5-6 was hidden in plain sight in my home. It took a long time before I "saw" this verse again and its words spoke to me.

Isn't it funny how we can grab onto the Word of God when things are good and call it true, but overlook it when things get messy? What verses have you known to be true but have ignored as the pains of life hid them under a blanket of dust? God never sends you into a battle that you aren't prepared, with His help, to fight. Dust off His Word, decide to trust Him and see what can happen!

7/30/20

*As I prepare to move to Virginia, Lord any battles we endure we are fully ready & equipped for. Thank you in advance for the truth that comes from your Word. Teach me to meditate on your word oh Lord my God*

## Prayer

*Father, help me to realize You have been speaking to me all along. I confess that some truths You revealed in Your Word and spoke to my heart long ago have become dust-covered with life. Allow me to experience You, Father, as the One who has already equipped me for the trials I am going through! In Jesus' name, amen.*

# DAY 6

## God is My Support

2 Samuel 22:19

*His divine power has given us everything we need for a godly life through our knowledge of Him who called us by His own glory and goodness. Through these He has given us His very great and precious promises, so that through them you may participate in the divine nature, having escaped the corruption in the world...*

2 Peter 1:3-4

What is your "knowledge of Him"? Do you believe that God is a good and glorious Father when life is going well, but doubt it when life is not? The way in which you react to situations is directly related to who you believe God really is.

Maybe you know Him as the Healer because He healed you, but you doubt He will provide for you. Perhaps you know Him as the provider but doubt He will vindicate you. If you don't see God working or don't believe He will show up in your need, you won't have faith in Him.

Don't let the corruption of this world tarnish the promises of God. If circumstances turned out differently than you had hoped, don't doubt God's goodness. Press through. Seek Him in your unresolved trials. Make the decision that God is good and His promises are for you. You will experience God and His divine nature!

## Prayer

*Father, I ask for faith to cling to the promise that You are a good God. I pray that no matter how things appear or how I feel, I will be determined to experience Your goodness. With Your help, I refuse to be overcome by my difficult situation. Help me to wait for You. It may take time. It may be very hard. But give me faith and courage to make a "no matter what" decision that You are good and that Your promises are true. I trust You to guide me through this and reveal Your true self to me. In Jesus' name, amen.*

# DAY 7

# God is the Lord Our Maker

Psalm 95:6

*Your eyes saw my unformed body; all the days ordained for me were written in Your book before one of them came to be.*

Psalm 139:16

Have you stopped to think that the Creator of the Universe *knows* you? He has known you since before you were even formed. Your Heavenly Father sees you intricately and thoroughly.

He declares the end from the beginning (Isaiah 46:10), knows the number of hairs on your head (Luke 12:7), and He will make perfect all that concerns you (Psalm 138:8). Nothing surprises Him. As we grasp the reality of being intimately known and deeply loved by God, we can begin to trust that He cares. Every detail of our lives matters to Him. He isn't shocked by our situations; He wants to be invited into them.

He wants to reveal His character in your circumstance. He desires for you to experience Him and His deep adoration for you. As you face your challenge today, thank God that it is an opportunity for Him to show you how much He values you.

## Prayer

*Jesus, help me rest in the assurance that You know everything about me. You know how I think and feel. You understand everything I have been through. I pray, Holy Spirit, for You to guide me into the Truth that I matter, and that I am significant. I am chosen (John 15:16), and I am accepted (Romans 15:7). My days are ordained by You (Psalm 139:16 NIV). You will never leave me nor forsake me (Deuteronomy 31:6). I praise You that Your presence and promises will guide me every step of the way! In Jesus' name, amen.*

# DAY 8

# God is the Lord Who Heals You.

Exodus 15:26

> *Is anyone among you suffering? Let him pray.*
> *Is anyone cheerful? Let him sing praise. Is anyone among you sick? Let him call for the elders of the church, and let them pray over him, anointing him with oil in the name of the Lord.*
> *And the prayer of faith will save the one who is sick, and the Lord will raise him up.*
> *And if he has committed sins, he will be forgiven.*
>
> James 5:13-15

You should never suffer alone. You are part of the body of Christ and we all need each other. Keeping your suffering to yourself isolates you and allows the enemy to work his ways into your thoughts and then your actions. You may feel like you are the only one who has your problem, or that no one understands. Do you have people you trust who will pray with you? If not, know that I am praying!

I distinctly remember when I was diagnosed with an ovarian tumor. The attending doctor (not my regular one) felt compelled to share the worst-case scenario with me. Had I been listening to her completely, I would have felt more scared than I was. However, I tuned her out right after the words, "You have a tumor…" The rest sounded like the teacher from the *Peanuts* --- "Wah-wah -wah." I knew that I needed "my people."

My dear friends prayed with me and battled against this invasion. I was anointed with oil and I continued to speak God's promises of healing over my body. The day before surgery, no tumor was found. I give all glory to God!

Now, I know that you may be thinking of someone who wasn't healed despite fervent prayer. It is a mystery we don't understand. What I do know is that in all situations, God will show up in some way. He will reveal the nature of His goodness even when the outcome isn't what we hoped it would be. I was able to trust Him because of my past experiences with Him, and I would have continued to trust Him even if I wasn't physically healed. Whether you need physical, emotional, or spiritual healing, Jesus died for all of it. Isaiah 53:5 says, "By His wounds, we are healed."

## Prayer

*Lord, please connect me with "my people," faith-filled friends who will encourage me and pray for me, reminding me of Your promises. Father, send laborers from the field to help carry the burdens I can't bear alone. Let me experience You through others. In Jesus' name, amen.*

# DAY 9

# God is the Lord Who Provides

Genesis 22:14

*He who supplies seed to the sower and bread for food will provide and multiply your seed for sowing and increase the harvest of your righteousness. You will be enriched in every way to be generous in every way, which through us will produce thanksgiving to God.*

2 Corinthians 9:10-11

All of your resources come from God. He supplies your every need. As you share these resources, such as time, love, compassion, service, finances, and prayer with others, you produce a harvest for His glory. The Bible tells us "a man reaps what he sows" (Galatians 6:7).

There should be a desire to reap good things. During a hard season, if you would focus on *whatever* it is you can be thankful for, then give to or serve others, you will be enriched in every way. There is nothing sweeter than encouraging someone who needs encouragement. It is OK to admit you need it too.

One of my favorite activities was to walk with a friend during a time we were both waiting on God. We would take turns recalling Scripture to encourage each other. Faith comes from hearing and hearing through the word of Christ (Romans 10:17). By the end of our walks, we would both be really empowered. What seemed like mountains in our lives became molehills as we spoke

God's Word over our circumstances.

We became thankful for our all-knowing, all-powerful God. We were excited that He was working on our behalf whether we could see it or not. Hope replaced hopelessness. Not to mention, if two or more agree, it will be done for them (Matthew 18:19).

## Prayer

*Lord, I praise You for all the good things in my life. There are many things to be thankful for. Bring these things to my mind; shift my thoughts to them.*

*Help me to reach out to another who is also in need. Help me be a source of encouragement to someone today. Even if it is a simple smile, it can make all the difference in someone's day. Help me, Father, to give to another what I desire for myself. Discouragement will flee, and hope will arise for me as I do unto others as I would have them do for me (Luke 6:31). In Jesus' name, amen.*

# DAY 10

# God is Compassionate and Gracious

Exodus 34:6

*And we know that for those who love God all things work together for good, for those who are called according to his purpose.*

Romans 8:28

When you have been hit with a discouraging or painful situation, it is difficult to see how any good can come from it. It often doesn't make sense. To be brutally honest, many of us don't care about whatever good may happen in the future. We would rather not have pain, heartache, or fear *now*. However, choosing to trust in God will give you a peace that someday this troubling experience will serve a useful purpose. It doesn't mean that what happened is good; it means that God will give a crown of beauty for ashes (Isaiah 61:3). You just need to let Him.

When my husband and I hit rock bottom in our marriage and began discussing divorce, no one could have told me that God would work that for good. By being determined to follow God and trust Him, though, the miraculous happened. It wasn't easy, and it wasn't overnight.

Since then, God has given me the opportunity to encourage countless women. Women who wanted to quit just like I wanted to. Because of my struggle, I know how many of these ladies feel.

I understand the fear and hopelessness. I also know the power of a loving God. I have experienced on numerous occasions what can happen when you trust Him. His redemptive power is the sweetest victory over the enemy who comes to steal, kill, and destroy (John 10:10) that I can think of!

## Prayer

*Holy Spirit, comfort me today. Grant me the peace that surpasses all understanding (Philippians 4:7). Increase my faith to know with certainty that You are with me, even in this storm. Jesus, help me, heal me, and use me in a mighty way to help others for Your glory. Work this trial for good as Your Word promises, so I can show others how You helped me. In Jesus' name, amen.*

# DAY 11

# God is the God Who Sees Me

Genesis 16:13

*He who planted the ear, does he not hear?*
*He who formed the eye, does he not see?*

Psalm 94:9

Do you think your prayers fall on deaf ears? Do you feel that God has forgotten you or doesn't notice what is happening? Does He see the good you are doing, or notice the bad that someone else is doing? Yes, He does.

When I was about 25 years old, I was depressed and felt that there was no hope to go on. A friend told me that God had written my name in "His Book" and that it had been recorded there since the beginning of time. I didn't know what that even meant. In my darkest hour, I asked God to show me a sign if He cared and if I mattered to Him. I knew I needed a miracle to help me, but had no expectations of receiving one.

A few days later my grandmother (who knew nothing of my plea) came to give me a gift, something she had found in her home. It was my great-grandfather's World War One New Testament Bible. My great-grandfather died when I was 12. Inside the front cover he had written, "To Lisa. Love, Nana, and G.G. Used during WWI." My name truly was in HIS Book! God *did* care. God cared enough to know that 13 years after my "G.G." wrote my name in "HIS Book," I would ask God if I mattered to Him. Take heart: You, my friend, matter to God too!

## Prayer

*Lord, I pray today that You would make Yourself known to me tangibly. You hear me, God; You see me, and You care. Would You give me a special message of encouragement today? Help me to experience how personal and detailed You really are! In Jesus' name, amen.*

# DAY 12

## God, the Lord is Peace

Judges 6:24

> *Behold, how good and pleasant it is when brothers dwell in unity!*
>
> Psalm 133:1

A majority of our stressors involve other people. God's plan for us, though, is to live in peace with each other. People will fail you. You will fail people. Deciding to let an offense not stick to you but, instead, handing it over to Jesus, is how you can show His grace to others. In addition, it empowers you.

A mature Christ-follower will choose the goodness of peace. This doesn't mean you ignore sin. It doesn't mean you should never speak up. It doesn't mean being a doormat and getting walked on. It means that you rely on the strength of Jesus to indicate that you value relationship and unity over strife. Romans 12:18 says, "If possible, so far as it depends on you, live peaceably with all." It is so easy to take offense, but I believe you can be a peaceable person and experience the power of God in your relationships!

## Prayer

*Holy Spirit, I pray for a fresh filling of grace and faith today. I ask for the fruits of Your Spirit (Galatians 5:22-23) to be evident in my life. Use me to be an example to others, to forgive quickly, love compassionately and to live in peace with others so much as it depends on me. When I feel that I can't do it, please bring Philippians 4:13 to my memory. Remind me that, "I can do all things through Him who strengthens me!" In Jesus' name, amen.*

# DAY 13

## God is the Strength of My Heart

Psalm 73:26

*Fear not, for I am with you; be not dismayed, for I am your*
*God; I will strengthen you, I will help you,*
*I will uphold you with my righteous right hand.*

Isaiah 41:10

Most of us fear the unknown, especially when our expectations or dreams have been shattered. We expect more of the same to occur. It can be paralyzing, or can even cause us to choose a harmful but *familiar* path over a way that leads to potential joy and healing. Knowing that God is with you, that He is never surprised at what is happening, and that He will hold you and strengthen you, brings a calmness to your time of waiting. The more you calm yourself in His presence and meditate on His character, the less fearful you will become. Also, remembering how He has moved on your behalf in past situations should encourage you that He will move in this one too!

## Prayer

*Father God, Your Word says that perfect love casts out fear (1 John 4:18). I ask for a fresh revelation of Your perfect love today. As Jesus told Peter to ignore the wind and the waves and keep his eyes on Him, I ask for the faith to do that too. Allow me to experience You as my protector, defender, and guide. Turn any dismay I have into joy, because of who You are and because of what You have planned for me. I praise You and thank You for holding me up and strengthening me. Praise You, Lord, for what You are doing on my behalf even if I can't see it or I don't understand it. In Jesus' name, amen!*

# DAY 14

# God is a Mighty God

Jeremiah 32:18

> *But he said to me, "My grace is sufficient for you, for my power is made perfect in weakness." Therefore, I will boast all the more gladly of my weaknesses, so that the power of Christ may rest upon me.*
>
> 2 Corinthians 12:9

The only way to know the power of God in your weakness is to let Him be the power. Panic never helped anyone. Worry never brings about a positive result. What if you were honest with God and told Him you were weak in this given situation? He knows that anyway. When you invite God into your circumstances, everything changes. Even if nothing visibly or outwardly changes, everything changes because He is working in you. The way you view the mountain in front of you, will change. As you watch Him provide for you, your faith will strengthen. If God says His grace is sufficient, then it is! Are you willing to admit your weakness and relinquish your need for control to The One who offers you His power in your life?

## Prayer

*Lord, I am weak. I praise You for Your grace, which You promise me is sufficient. I surrender control of things that worry me. Your Word says that You did not give me a spirit of fear, but of love, power, and self-control (2 Timothy 1:7). I ask to experience Your love, peace and mighty power today. Thank You that the power of Jesus will rest in me and on me when I need it. I ask this for Your Glory, Lord. In Jesus' name, amen.*

# DAY 15

## God is Near

Psalm 145:18

> ***The Lord is near to the brokenhearted and
> saves the crushed in spirit.***
>
> Psalm 34:18

Has your spirit been crushed by something that has turned your entire life upside down? Or maybe, instead, you have been defeated in a small area in your life. Even a tiny disappointment can become a shadow of sadness that, if left unchecked, can creep into the good areas of our lives like a dark cloud.

I remember feeling very much alone in my pain because of a ministry wound. I blamed God and felt utterly abandoned by Him. Maybe something causes you think the same way. The truth, though, whether we feel it or not, is that God is close to us. The enemy comes to steal, kill, and destroy but Jesus came that we may have a full life (John 10:10).

Blaming God for what you are going through plays right into the enemy's hands. If he can destroy your relationship with God by creating heartache, then he wins a battle. Of course, we know that he has already lost the war because Jesus died and rose again, but that doesn't mean he won't try to sabotage you.

Trusting that Jesus relates to your pain and knows your heartache begins the healing process for your crushed spirit. It may take time. Be determined to cling to Him and His Word. He is near to all who call on Him (Psalm 145:18). Let Him breathe love, life, and hope into your heart. God did not bring this situation on you, but He will carry you through it!

## Prayer

*Jesus, I feel lost and abandoned at times. Although I may feel alone, I ask the Holy Spirit to fill me with Your love. Your Word says You will never leave me or forsake me (Deuteronomy 31:6). Mend my broken heart. I ask for Your powerful blood, Jesus, to pour into my wounds and heal me, revive me, and strengthen me. Help me to refuse the enemy's plot steal my joy and keep me from trusting You. I ask You to pick me up and hold me. "Let me hear in the morning of Your steadfast love, for in You I trust. Make me know the way I should go, for to You I lift up my soul" (Psalm 143:8). In Jesus' name, amen.*

# DAY 16

## God is the Lord My Rock

Psalm 28:1

*Be still, and know that I am God. I will be exalted among the nations; I will be exalted in the earth!*

Psalm 46:10

Be still. Be at rest in God. Have confidence that everything is in His hands and under His feet (Ephesians 1:22). Your circumstances are not beyond the reach of the Creator of the Universe. Often, we understand this truth in our heads, but does it really make us feel better?

If I were to be totally honest with you, that knowledge doesn't always soothe me. When I am waiting for something and want a resolution immediately, on my own time, being still doesn't feel good at all. If I am still, I don't have control. I need to have a plan. I need to figure things out. I have to have a solution.

The Message translation of Psalm 46:10 says it well: "Step out of the traffic! Take a long, loving look at me, your High God…"

When you take matters into your own hands trying to control things, it's like standing on a four-lane highway during rush hour. You're dodging fast-moving cars. You feel overwhelmed and unsafe. Your eyes, thoughts, and emotions are darting back and forth; there is no peace.

You're searching for that break in the traffic so you can run to safety and finally breathe easy. But the verse directs our attention to another route: be still and know that I am God. Step out of the traffic. Calm yourself in God's presence. Focus your attention on Him and *know* your High God.

God will reveal different aspects of His character as you invite Him into your situations. You will know Him in a deeper, more intimate way. This will be the greatest gift He will give you while you wait.

## Prayer

*Lord, help me step out of the traffic of my life and take a long, loving look at You. Grant me peace. Show me Your goodness in this. I believe that as I am still, I will experience You. And when I experience You, I can be still. In Jesus' name, amen.*

# DAY 17

# God is My Righteous Father

John 17:25

*Charm is deceitful, and beauty is vain, but a woman who fears the Lord is to be praised. Give her of the fruit of her hands, and let her works praise her in the gates.*

Proverbs 31:30-31

A woman who fears the Lord is a woman who has reverence for Him. When you experience God for who He really is, you are in awe of His tender mercy toward you. Choose to trust Him, and you will experience Him more profoundly. Reverence holds the hand of trust. Surrendering to the righteous Father in Heaven and obeying Him blesses you with fruitfulness. This is also a form of worship that reaches heaven.

Maybe you have had a past encounter that showed you that you mattered to God. You knew He "saw" you. If you are discouraged today, remember what He did for you before, and then be in awe. Give Him praise. Worship Him as the King of Kings, the Lord of Lords, and the Rock in whom you take refuge (Psalm 18:2). Godly strength and dignity are qualities that last, and for them you will be "praised in the gates."

## Prayer

*Lord, I praise You and thank You for all that you have done for me. I confess I am discouraged today. I choose to remember when You came through for me in the past. Help me to trust that You are working behind the scenes on my behalf. Forgive me for doubting and for being impatient. Holy Spirit, continue to work out Your fruit in me (Galatians 5:22) so that I glorify God in all that I do. Keep me in awe of You, Lord. Give me the fruit of my hands and let my works be pleasing to You. In Jesus' name, amen.*

# DAY 18

## The Lord is a God of Retribution

Jeremiah 51:56

*Therefore, do not throw away your confidence, which has a great reward. For you have need of endurance, so that when you have done the will of God, you may receive what is promised.*

Hebrews 10:35-36

Confidence is a certainty in someone or something. It is a firm trust. How often do you become exasperated while waiting for things to turn around? Or, you hold onto hope only to feel as if the promise or solution is like a dangling carrot, so you give up. What drives some people to stick with something and others to give up? Think about matters you have seen through, even when it was very hard. Think of things you readily quit when the going got tough. Why did you choose to commit or quit?

If you have confidence in the God of the impossible (Matthew 19:26), it exercises your faith like a muscle and it becomes stronger. You are given the gift of endurance. Once you press through, you can see the hand of God. You will see how He led you, sustained you, and came through for you. Stay the course and receive what He has promised you.

## Prayer

*Father in Heaven, I ask Your Holy Spirit to fill me with newfound faith today. I ask You to fan the flame of faith in my heart. Give me determination and endurance to do Your will in my situation. I praise You for being the God of the impossible (Matthew 19:26). I celebrate what You are doing and how You are growing me in this process. Your Word says, "If God is for me, no one can stand against me" (Romans 8:31). Thank You for standing with me! I declare a firm trust in You, the Creator of the Universe and Lover of my soul! In Jesus' name, amen.*

# DAY 19

## God is Abundant in Power

Psalm 147:5

*Then he said to me, "… Not by might, nor by power, but by my Spirit", says the Lord of hosts.*

Zechariah 4:6

Do you feel discouraged or overwhelmed by what you are facing? Are you relying on your own strengths, abilities, and talents to get through this waiting season? Do you feel alone in doing what you need to do? As we rely on the Spirit of God, we invite the supernatural into the natural. He gives us renewed strength, inspired ideas, divine wisdom and a peace that surpasses all understanding. You are not alone when you have the power of God going ahead of you! Ask the Holy Spirit, the Helper (John 14:26), to do what He does best!

# Prayer

*Holy Spirit, I invite You into my situation. I praise You for being the Spirit of counsel and of power (Isaiah 11:2) and the Spirit of wisdom and revelation (Ephesians 1:17). Align my will with Your will. Make my foundation firm in Jesus Christ.*

*Build my life into the purposes God created for me (Eph. 2:10). Guide me to my destiny, that my life would be a house of praise (1 Peter 2:5). May I walk in Your power so that I might draw many to You, Lord. In Jesus' name, amen.*

# DAY 20

# God is My Strong Deliverer

Psalm 140:7

*Blessed is the man who remains steadfast under trial, for when he has stood the test, he will receive the crown of life, which God has promised to those who love him.*

James 1:12

Everyone loves an award or a reward. When you work hard, it is so encouraging to receive recognition for your dedication and effort. What if you stopped looking at earthly rewards and considered your spiritual ones?

I remember back when I was deeply discouraged from not seeing positive changes in my marriage. I felt I was giving it my all, obeying God by being respectful, and it wasn't helping me at all, or so it seemed. There was no visible or palpable reward for all my sacrifice.

Finally, I arrived at a place of total surrender. I remember saying, "Lord it doesn't matter what it looks like here on earth. I will do what you have asked me to do. Even if nothing changes in my marriage, I will do what You ask. I will be the wife you've called me to be, regardless of the outcome on earth. I trust You will bless me in eternity."

If you stop and think about it, eternity is...eternal! Stand firm in your trial so you can receive the crown of life, the blessings in eternity that last forever. Don't give up when you can't see an immediate reward.

It wasn't long after my total surrender to God that things changed in my marriage. It was as if He said, "Now I have you where I want you." Regardless, however, of the outcome in this life, we should set our sights on eternal things, as they last forever.

## Prayer

*Jesus, You are my eternal reward. No matter what I face in my life, I know that because of Your sacrifice on the cross, I will be with You forever. But let that not be enough. Change me. Grow me. Use me. Holy Spirit, help me to remain steadfast in trials. Bring to the surface whatever You want to heal in me and deliver me from. Help me to not focus on circumstances that are temporary, but to fix my eyes on You, Jesus. Use me to point others also going through trials, to You. I trust that my obedience will be rewarded in heaven, and I thank You that You are a rewarder of those who diligently seek You (Hebrews 11:6). In Jesus' name, amen.*

# DAY 21

## God is My Hope and Trust

Psalm 71:5

> *Cast your burden on the Lord, and he will sustain you;*
> *he will never permit the righteous to be moved.*
>
> Psalm 55:22

We worry, we examine, we attempt to control, or worse, we manipulate. We fix whatever we can to make life better. We have hours of conversations about what to do and what not to do. The more we talk, the more anxious we can become. The more people we talk to, the more confused we can get. Many times, we forget to go to the Lord first. Yes, it is valuable to receive wisdom from others, but we need to seek God first.

Sometimes people just want conversation; they aren't really looking for counsel. People can fall into the trap of finding others who tell them what they want to hear and who agree with what they have already decided. If they find agreement, they feel their burden will be lighter; they feel validated and understood. But if this is our strategy, will it help produce change?

What do you do then if your situation becomes worse? The Father of Compassion (2 Corinthians 1:3), who is never taken by surprise, is waiting for you. Taking your burden to the Lord first will help immensely. He knows your heart anyway. Talk to

Him. Yell and cry if you have to. Then sit and listen. Listen for the still small voice to speak to your heart.

Ask Him to highlight godly people who can help, if that is what is needed. People who will seek Him with you. Don't waste precious time whining and complaining to people who can't really help you. Let God sustain you so that your faith will not be moved!

## Prayer

*Lord, thank You that I can cast my burdens on You. I ask for You to sustain me (Psalm 54:4) in this storm. I thank You that You promise the righteous will not be moved. I stand on that promise. Holy Spirit I ask You for peace and wisdom. I ask You to highlight someone who will help me with godly wisdom if that is what I need. I repent of worry, doubt, and faithless talk. You have me, and You will guide and protect me. I praise You for that. In Jesus' name, amen.*

# DAY 22

## God Can Do More Than We Ask or Imagine

Ephesians 3:20

> *No unbelief made him waver concerning the promise of God, but he grew strong in his faith as he gave glory to God, fully convinced that God was able to do what He had promised.*
>
> Romans 4:20-21

God does not bring calamity and chaos into our lives. A good Father would never do that. Consider your trial as an invitation for God to reveal Himself in this sinful world. Romans 4:20-21 talks about Abraham, who is known for his faith. He trusted God. Even in the most impossible situations, his faith never faltered. God promised that he would be the father of many nations, yet asked him to sacrifice his miracle son with Sarah, through whom that promise was to be fulfilled. Still, Abraham knew God could keep His promise; all Abraham had to do was be obedient. God intervened, spared Isaac and fulfilled the promise to Abraham.

As you decide, like Abraham, to stand firm on God's promises, you become convinced that God is able to do what He promises He can do. He can do more than you think He can. Have you considered that He is at work, but you just can't see it right now?

Instead of focusing on what isn't happening, give God glory in this season for what He *is* doing that you can't see. Thank Him for what His Word says that He can do. Abraham witnessed fruit from his faithfulness, and it is fruit that continues on even today. Stay grounded in God's good character and promises. He can do more than you can even imagine. Remain faithful. Then you will never have to wonder, "What if I would have trusted God?"

## Prayer

*Father God, I give You glory today. I praise You for being my ever-present help in trouble (Psalm 46:1). I may not understand how You are going to work this situation out, but I choose to believe that You will. Grant me the faith of Abraham. Holy Spirit, help me remove any unbelief I may have in God's goodness and faithfulness. In Jesus' name, amen.*

# DAY 23

## God is the Father of Compassion

2 Corinthians 1:3

*The steadfast love of the Lord never ceases; his mercies never come to an end; they are new every morning; great is your faithfulness. "The Lord is my portion," says my soul, "therefore I will hope in him."*

Lamentations 3:22-24

It is easy to assume that God has forgotten you when things aren't going the way you think they should. Though you may you feel unloved or unlovable, His Word says His love never ceases. When was the last time you reflected on how God's love for you never ends?

If His love is never-ending and His mercies are new every day, then you can have hope for tomorrow. You can have faith that He will help you with whatever you are facing, and have hope that this season will not last forever. You will have confidence that He has a bigger plan, one that is good, even if you can't see it now. Anchor your faith in the steadfast love the Lord has for you. Allow Him to be enough, and it will renew your strength.

## Prayer

*Holy Spirit, I ask for a deeper revelation of God's perfect love. 1 John 4:18 says, "His perfect love casts out fear."*

*I confess I am afraid, which causes me to doubt You. I am thankful, though, that Your mercies are new every day. As I place my trust in You, I know my heart and my perception of my situation will change. Even if my circumstances don't change the way I would want, my perception can change when I ask You to lead me. Open the eyes of my heart to see You in a new way today. In Jesus' name, amen.*

# DAY 24

## God is a Stronghold in Time of Trouble

Psalm 9:9

> *The Lord is good, a stronghold in the day of trouble;*
> *he knows those who take refuge in him.*

Nahum 1:7

When you allow your circumstances to teach you more about God, you learn how to take refuge in Him. As you seek Him for protection from your troubles, the fear of the unknown lessens. God desires a surrendered heart! Relinquish control and hand your burdens to Him. He will direct you as well as protect you. The Lord is good. Any situation you face, even if it's painful or unbearable, is an opportunity for God to show you His goodness. He will show you that you can run to Him for safety in the midst of the storm. It comes down to a simple decision. You need to be willing to run *to* Him, instead of running from Him.

## Prayer

*Lord Jesus, Your sacrifice on the cross was the most loving and powerful thing You could have done for me. There is no human explanation for why You chose to do that, other than a love for me beyond what I can understand. Ultimately, it is the only proof I need that You are good.*

*Because of that Truth, help me to believe that Your intentions for me are always good no matter what is happening. You will work my current situation out for my good, as I rely on You. I choose to believe You are my stronghold and I can rely on You. Help me to run to You and not from You. Show me when to be still and when to take action. I give You thanks and praise for what You are doing on my behalf, even if I can't see it right now. In Jesus' name, amen.*

# DAY 25

## God is a Source of Strength

Isaiah 28:6

*Seek the Lord and his strength;*
*seek his presence continually.*

1 Chronicles 16:11

People spend countless hours and sleepless nights worrying. I have heard it said that worrying is like a rocking chair. You keep moving, but you don't go anywhere. Likewise, it is a waste of time to worry about what may never happen. Today, be determined to seek God and His strength. How? Commit to memory the scriptures that say, "He is the God of the impossible" (Luke 18:27), and "He can do more than you can think, ask, imagine or dream" (Ephesians 3:20). Believe that He is for you, not against you (Romans 8:31). Consider Him a stronghold in times of trouble (Nahum 1:7). As you reflect on these truths, sit quietly and invite His presence to minister to you. He longs to make Himself known to you. Seek Him, and you will find Him when you seek Him with all of your heart (Jeremiah 29:13).

## Prayer

*Holy Spirit, I ask for You to lead me into Truth; the Truth that the Lord is my strength. Fill me with Your presence as I seek Your face, Father God. Help me to learn about You and to trust in Your mighty power. Rearrange my priorities to seek Your presence continually. As I rest with You, Lord, may it encourage me to be completely surrendered to You. May I grasp the wisdom that I am not alone, because the same Spirit who raised Christ from the dead lives in me (Romans 8:11). May I understand that I am not powerless, because my hope includes God's incomparably great power, which He exerted when he raised Christ from the dead (Ephesians 1:19-20). I stand on Your Word, that with You all things are possible! In Jesus' name, amen.*

# DAY 26

# God is the One Who Sustains Me

Psalm 54:4

*For the sake of Christ, then, I am content with weaknesses, insults, hardships, persecutions, and calamities. For when I am weak, then I am strong.*

2 Corinthians 12:10

Contentment is a state of satisfaction and happiness. Can you honestly say that you have peace when you face trouble? Discouragement can easily sweep you off of your feet. You feel disillusioned, and sometimes quite overwhelmed. The apostle Paul met many trials, yet he proclaimed his contentment. How?

Contentment was only possible for him because of his awareness of who God really is. He had seen God show up for him time and time again. His faith in God was more significant than his faith in himself or his circumstances. When you are weak, you can become strong because of a heavenly Father you can trust. He is your refuge. As you surrender to the Lord, you invite His strength into your life. His power is revealed. The more God shows up mightily on your behalf, the easier it is to have contentment in future trials. You will then strengthen your trust in His power.

# Prayer

*Jesus, for Your glory, I lay my weaknesses at the foot of the cross. With the help of Your Holy Spirit, I acknowledge Your power and Your strength when hardships come. I trust You, that it is another chance for You to reveal Yourself to me in a new way. You promise that You will never leave me nor forsake me (Hebrews 13:5). When I feel weak, I believe that I am strong because of You. Uplift me with Your mighty hand as I move forward in our journey together. Grant me Your peace, the peace that surpasses all understanding. Help me to know that I can be content in this weakness because of Your strength. In Jesus' name, amen.*

# DAY 27

## God is My Confidence

Psalm 71:5

*Do not be anxious about anything, but in everything by prayer and supplication with thanksgiving let your requests be made known to God.*

Philippians 4:6

Hopefully when you were a young child and something distressing happened, there was someone older and wiser present who made you feel at ease. You gained a peace about things because someone else was "handling it". Maybe it was a parent, a grandparent, teacher, or that friend who could solve any problem.

Although adulthood brings about more responsibilities and more troubles, we still have someone we can rely on. You don't need to handle things yourself. The Bible says that if you need wisdom, you should ask, and it will be given to you (James 1:5). Repent of anxiety, which is rooted in fear. 1 John 4:18 says that God's perfect love casts out fear.

Ask God for a deeper revelation of His perfect love. Present your requests to Him and thank Him for hearing you.

Praise Him for being the problem solver in your life. He is the one to run to. As you trust in His goodness, your future trials won't be enveloped in useless anxiety. They will be wrapped in His powerful love, wisdom, and guidance.

## Prayer

*Father, forgive me for being anxious and for looking at my problem more than I look at Your greatness. Help me to focus on who You are and who I am in You, instead of on this situation. Show me when my mind wanders off of Your promises and onto my troubles. Holy Spirit, open the eyes of my heart to receive a deeper revelation of God's perfect love for me.*

*I give thanks to You, Lord, for giving me wisdom generously and for hearing my prayers. Open my spiritual ears to hear what You are saying to me. In Jesus' name, amen.*

# DAY 28

## God is the Eternal King

Jeremiah 10:10

*So we fix our eyes not on what is seen, but on what is unseen since what is seen is temporary, but what is unseen is eternal.*

2 Corinthians 4:18

I remember growing very tired when I was trying to "do good". Despite my efforts in doing what God asked me to do, I didn't see any changes in my circumstances. Clearly, I was stumbling in my faith walk, because scripture tells us not to grow weary (Galatians 6:9).

It was in my emotional weariness that I was finally able to surrender. I did not quit, but I fully surrendered to God. To be honest, I was exhausted. I remember saying, "Lord, I want to do what You want me to do. Regardless of the outcome here on earth, I will do what You ask of me. Even if nothing changes, I will trust that you will bless my obedience in eternity. Eternity is a lot longer than my life here on earth." Not long after that everything changed! Praise God!

Don't focus on the temporary things of this world no matter how long they seem to last. Eternity is infinite. As you do what God asks of you, you will receive His rewards. 2 Corinthians 4:17 says, "For momentary, light affliction is producing for us an eternal weight of glory far beyond all comparison…"

Don't let your hearts be troubled. Christ has gone ahead and prepared a place for you (John 14:1-3). Focus on the eternal glory God has for you. Don't waver from it. Surrender and keep your eye on the eternal prize.

## Prayer

*Lord God, although I may stumble in my faith and at times grow tired, help me to fix my eyes on You. Help me to be unwavering in my trust of Your faithfulness and to trust Your timing. Remind me to focus on eternal blessings instead of temporary comforts. Give me glimpses of Your glory to spur me on. I long to hear, "Well done, good and faithful servant. You have been faithful over a little; I will set you over much. Enter into the joy of your master" (Matthew 25:21). Help me to honor You with my life on earth so that I may be fully rewarded in heaven. In Jesus' name, amen.*

# DAY 29

## God is a Refuge for His People

Joel 3:16

*We wait in hope for the Lord; he is
our help and our shield.*

Psalm 33:20

How does one wait well?

Have hope in the Lord. Set aside your doubts and fears. Relinquish your need to control situations. Decide to focus on God. Sometimes we need to get out of our own way so God can move.

He is the miracle worker. He resurrects, restores, rebuilds, strengthens and creates. The very words of His mouth bring life. As you wait on Him with the hope of what He can do, you have an assurance that you will be well taken care of. God is your help and your shield. Isn't that what you look for in times of trouble?

Psalm 33:20, above, promises that He is protecting you. Focus on who He really is. Build your faith in the character of God. Be sure it is based on His infallible Word and not on a negative experience. As you do, the joy of the Lord will be your strength (Nehemiah 8:10).

## Prayer

*Father, I thank You that You are my help and my shield. What more do I need? You cover me. You know the answers to every problem. Nothing shakes You. Because of this, I set my heart to wait in hope, with eager expectation of what You long to do in my life. Holy Spirit, grant me newfound faith to set this hope in my heart. Reveal more about who You are, Lord, as I wait. Let me experience You in a powerful way, all for Your glory. In Jesus' name, amen.*

# DAY 30

# God is My Redeemer

Psalm 78:35

*For by grace you have been saved through faith. And this is not your own doing; it is the gift of God, not a result of works, so that no one may boast.*

Ephesians 2:8-9

Your salvation is free. It costs you nothing, but it did cost Jesus everything. Just as you have the faith that grace has saved you, have faith that God desires a continued, growing relationship with you. He isn't a "nice to meet you, now move along" kind of God. He desires you to be in deep fellowship with Him. He wants a relationship that involves Him in your highs and in your lows, in the good times and in the bad. It doesn't make sense to trust that you are saved, yet not trust the One who saved you, does it? Don't allow situations that you face cause you to undermine the valuable relationship God, your heavenly Father, wants to have with you.

He gives you the gifts of salvation, eternal life, the power of the Holy Spirit, spiritual fruits, spiritual gifts and all of His promises. You are a co-heir with Christ (Romans 8:17 NIV) and what is His is yours. Don't let your thoughts take you away from the Truth that in every moment of your life God is a merciful and gracious God. He is slow to anger, and abounding in steadfast love and faithfulness (Exodus 34:6). He is not just the

Redeemer of your soul, as important as that is. He is your Redeemer in all things!

## Prayer

*Lord, thank You for the free gift of grace for my salvation. Secure my feet firmly on the foundational truth that You who began a good work in me will bring it to completion (Philippians 1:6). You did not rescue me at the moment of my salvation to abandon me now. Forgive me if I have walked away from You. Thank You for never leaving me. Use my circumstances to show me Your goodness, to refine me and grow me, and to make me more like Jesus. Praise You for being my Redeemer, my Father, my Friend. In Jesus' name, amen.*

# Moving Forward

*He will cover you with His feathers, and under*
*His wings you will find refuge.*

Psalm 91:4

My passionate prayer for you is that you walk in the awareness of God's true character and have an unshakeable faith in who He really is. At the beginning of this 30-day journey together, I shared that the way in which we handle any situation, good or bad, is in direct relation to whom we believe God is. I know that as you have spent time with Him, praying Spirit-led prayers and allowing His Word to penetrate your heart, you have come to know Him better. Keep growing!

As you move forward in your life, pray that God uses all situations to reveal His goodness. You will never know the vastness of God's character this side of heaven, but that doesn't mean you should wait until eternity to start experiencing more of who He is.

God is a relational God and a loving Father. He promises to be with you every step of the way. He covers you and provides you refuge because He cares so deeply for you. A refuge is a shelter from danger or trouble. It is a sanctuary. We can't always escape trouble in our lives but, with God, we are safe in the midst of it. Jesus modeled this for us as He slept on a boat in a storm (Mark 4:37-41). God also promises to work even the worst of times for your good (Romans 8:28). We just need to let Him do that.

We may not understand why difficult things happen to us, but we can have faith in the God who does. Now, be still and experience God!

Blessings,

*Lisa*

LisaSheaMinistries.com

HowToWaitWell.com

# Only Through Jesus

We can only come to God the Father through the saving grace of His Son, Jesus. Jesus tells us, "I am the way, the truth and the life. No one comes to the Father except through me" (John 14:6). Scripture promises us that whoever calls on the name of the Lord will be saved (Romans 10:13). Jesus Himself said that if you come to Him, He will not cast you out (John 6:37). Jesus died and rose again so that we could be forgiven of our sins and be united in heaven with the Father, Son and Holy Spirit for eternity.

If you have never repented of your sins and said yes to receiving the saving grace of Jesus, it only takes a simple act of faith. Ask Jesus to forgive you and call on His name to be saved. Ask to be filled with the Holy Spirit to empower you to live the life Jesus died to give you.

# Devotional Themes

Confidence: Day 3,6,7,13,18,21,23,25,26,27,30

Doubt: Day 3,6,8,11,14,17,21,23,25,27,30

Discouragement: Day 1,2,9,10,17,19,20,21,26,30

Faithfulness: Day 1,5,6,9,10,12,13,18,21,22,23,26

Fear/Worry: Day 2,7,8,10,13,14,21,23,24,25,27,29,30

Overwhelmed: Day 4,15,16,19,26,30

Surrender/Obedience: Day 12,14,16,20,24,25,26,28

Made in the USA
Lexington, KY
07 November 2019